Prayer

A WAY OF LIFE

ELDER LARRY YOUNG

ISBN 978-1-0980-7227-8 (paperback)
ISBN 978-1-0980-7228-5 (digital)

Christian Faith Publishing, Inc.
832 Park Avenue
Meadville, PA 16335
www.christianfaithpublishing.com

Printed in the United States of America

Contents

Preface

Prayer should definitely be *a way of life*, especially for every born-again child of God. Prayer is a way of communicating with the Lord. It's a way of developing and maintaining a close, intimate relationship with the almighty. Prayer is the means of allowing God to know about our situations and circumstances that affect our everyday lives. Truly, prayer can be a beneficial asset to anyone who desires and needs God's immediate attention concerning certain matters.

Unfortunately, most people do not use this very reliable and helpful tool to their full advantage. Prayer to God seems to be the last resort or final option in our battle against many problems and troubles that we face every day. The Lord shouldn't be the very last option but rather the first means of help.

Prayer is like planting seeds in the soil, cultivating and watering that soil, and waiting for God to give the increase, which is an expected harvest. The least thing one could do is to faithfully make one's request known to God, then cultivate that prayer request with spiritual works of faith and searching and seeking for God's answer with patient endurance.

Remember, God could easily answer our prayers immediately. However, we must understand that he may not always answer right away. Just know that he is *sovereign*, and he does whatever he wants, whenever and however he wants to. He is never intimidated to do things exactly when we want *him* to do them. Because he is God, allow him permission do things only in his own time, in his own way, and according to his will.

Please understand that God knows the right time and the right way to handle all of our problems. We seriously need to learn how to trust his *divine* judgment, while fully recognizing that the all-wise *God* never makes a mistake.

I've learned throughout the years that prayer to God is not something to be taken lightly or deemed unimportant. We should not assume that God desires to hear from us only when we are in serious trouble and desperately in need of his help. Some even feel that God is only concerned about our "toughest problems" and is not at all interested in our meager "mediocre" setbacks.

I'll remind you that nothing could be farther from the truth; for not only is God concerned about our "giant" problems, but he also cares about our "smallest" matters as well. Please consider that he is truly a "*God* of compassion." When the everyday troubles and trials of life weigh you down, just tell Jesus. It's comforting to know that we can cast all our cares on him, for *he* cares for us (1 Peter 5–7).

God strongly desires an intimate relationship with his creation. He walked through the garden of Eden, continuously desiring fellowship and conversation with Adam and Eve. He wants to communicate with us. Oh, how *reassuring* it is to know that he really *likes* us!

Prayer will get God involved. When we pray, it makes the Lord feel that he is needed. He smiles and is eager and willing to come to our rescue when we diligently seek *him*. Please consider that prayer keeps our minds on God, and it continually makes us aware of his presence. Through consistent prayer, *we* show God that he is the only one that we, as believers, trust to solve our many problems and setbacks. Within our trust in him, we totally surrender to his own wisdom and ability to conquer our highest mountains and our deepest valleys.

Prayer causes us to realize that we can do nothing through our own weak and freshly abilities. Jesus said, "Without me, you can do nothing" (John 15:5). No matter how great our circumstances and troubles may be, remember there is "nothing" too hard for God (Jeremiah 32:17).

Actually, when one prays to the Lord, surrendering all into his hands, it reassures our faith in him when he hears and answers. His great faithfulness causes one's soul to declare that there is indeed a God that can do all things, even going above all that we could ever hope or imagine.

Please understand that prayer, like faith, moves God and causes *him* to react. Just to know that we need him and desire to hear from him truly touches his heart. Prayer is an effective medicine that heals the pains of sorrow, depression, loneliness, and despair; for a dose or two of daily prayers will surely make one healthy, wealthy, and wise.

Don't stop praying.

1

Have You Prayed Today?

In 2 Chronicles 7:14, it reads:

> If my people which are called by my name shall humble themselves and pray, and seek my face, and turn from their wicked ways; then will I hear from heaven, and will forgive their sins, and heal their land.

A man lost the head of a borrowed axe into the water. He was desperate and asked the prophet to pray that God would recover *it*. Who would ever imagine that God would care to recover a mere axe head? Because God cares for the smallest of things, he recovers *it*. He is always doing the miraculous, even in causing an axe head to *surface* (2 Kings 6:1–7).

Hebrews 11:6 reads: "But without faith it is impossible to please Him; for he that cometh to God must believe that He is, and that He is a rewarder of them that diligently seek Him."

We should always want God to get involved in everything we engage in, for God's intervention will make the difference between being happy with the outcome or being disappointed with the end result.

Please understand that there is nothing that he is oblivious to. He is well aware of all things and understands all situations, even our many temptations.

In 1 Corinthians 10:13, it reads:

> There hath no temptation taken you, but such as is common to man: but God is faithful, who will not suffer you to be tempted above that you are able; but will, with the temptation also make a way of escape, that you may be able to bear it.

He knows about all of your *shortcomings,* failures, and weaknesses. Hebrews 2:17–18 reads:

> Wherefore in all things it behooved Him to be made like unto His brethren, that He might be a faithful high priest in things pertaining to God, to make reconciliation for the sins of the people in that He Himself hath suffered being tempted, He is able to succor them that are tempted.

Hebrews 4:15 reads:

> For we have not an high priest which cannot be touched with the feeling of our infirmities; but was in all points tempted like as we are, yet without sin.

Isaiah 40:28 reads:

> Hast thou not known? Hast thou not heard, that the everlasting God, the Lord, the Creator of the ends of the earth, fainteth not, neither is weary? There is no searching of His understanding.

Luke 18:1 reads:

> And Jesus spoke this parable unto them,
> that men *ought* to always pray and not to faint.

Don't stop praying!

Please understand, dear hearts, that the enemy, the devil, doesn't want you to pray. He'll do any and everything he can to distract and deter your prayer life.

He'll tell you that you don't need to pray today. He'll say that you can always pray later. He'll even tell you that it's okay, go on to the store, and get that new outfit before someone else buys it; or perhaps, he'll say that your favorite show is about to come on and you certainly don't want to miss it. Please don't fall for his tricks and lies, for he is a deceiver and a liar, and we are not ignorant of his devices (2 Corinthians 2:11).

Yes, loved ones do indeed need some of your time, but so does God. The devil is strongly trying to distract you because he knows that your (*strength and power*) against him is in your intimate time with God (*your prayer life*).

Please continue to remind the Lord that we definitely need him every hour of the day and that we cannot make it without him. Our meditating thoughts should be constantly in God's nourishing presence. If we truly and sincerely need his presence and omnipotent power, then we should act like it and make him aware.

I truly believe the best way to start our day is on our knees. You may not be able to get to the church every morning, but one can always make a spiritual altar in one's bedroom, bathroom, automobile, office, or any other of your favorite quiet surroundings. After all, God is *omnipresent*. He is everywhere at all times (Selah).

Mark 10:46–52 tells us that "when" we pray, not "if" we pray, we should believe that we will receive what we ask of him. Blind Bartimaeus "asked" the Lord to restore his sight; "he believed," and *he* received his sight.

As the psalmist said, he is a "very present help." He's always there when we need him, for he's "never too late." And if he is late, it's on purpose and for our good. We should all agree that we are surpassed about with so great a "cloud of witnesses" that would tell us that God will never let us down.

Those witnesses would tell us, from their own personal experiences, that he's always *showed up on time*. The redeemed of the Lord should certainly say so (Psalms 107:2).

I truly believe that big decisions and all decisions deserve God's help, for his attention and intervention is very vital (1 Samuel 30).

King David had a major dilemma (real trouble), and just like in times past, he enquired of God as to what he should do, and as always, God answered him, and David was a man of like passionate faith as we are.

In other words, he was no different from one of us. The enemy had destroyed their homes and taken their families captive, but David knew what to do. David asked God for instruction, direction, and council. He did not want to make any decisions on his own. He was strongly aware that he needed God's all-wise and all-knowing divine intervention. I'm sure you would agree that we need to learn how to seek that same Godly intervention.

Let's gladly testify of his goodness and intervention into our situations. We could tell a dying world that the Lord Jesus is the answer to all of the troubles we face every day. By our own testimonies, we could encourage them to pray and seek God's face for help and relief, for the world needs someone to turn to.

My time in God's face reassures me and lets me know that everything is going to be all right. My prayer time is so essential to me just as the water and food that I need every day in order to survive. If I did not have a consistent prayer life, I believe I would simply give up hope and worry myself into painful distress and eventual destruction.

It may be very hard for you who doesn't have this type of relationship with God to really grasp and understand what I'm trying to relate to you. But I believe that if you would just keep listening to my testimonies found within these pages, you'll truly comprehend what I'm trying to say.

Why not practice every day, seeking God for more of *his Spirit, his holiness, his ways*, and *his godly nature*? Matthew 6:33 reads: "But, seek ye first the kingdom of God, and His righteousness; and all these things shall be added unto you."

A strong desire for his peace and his patience within our hearts is priceless. At all times, we should ask him to forgive us for our sins and transgressions against him and others, while yet asking him to help us to forgive those who may have been hurtful and offensive toward us.

Prayer just makes one feel better. Our day started in prayer will put God at the forefront and put our enemies on the defensive and fleeing because he is with us to fight all our battles. We have to believe that things we face during the day have already been conquered and defeated.

Our daily devotionals with God bring *unspeakable joy* to our entire day. Consistent prayer is *spiritual medicine* to our souls. It lifts us up and gives us hope and courage. It gives us the confidence and assurance that everything is going to be all right!

Sunrise prayer and dawning of the day prayer makes you smile, helps you think positive, and causes you to have faith to believe in the Lord and to really trust him.

Have you prayed today?

2

Gethsemane

Do you ever ask yourself on what to do in certain dilemmas? What do you do when certain troubles and crisis arise? How do you handle real turbulent times? When huge and disastrous problems invade your peaceful and calm surroundings, do you panic or seek help from the Lord? The answer is "Gethsemane," the place of prayer, *the strengthening place.*

Sometimes, we don't know what to pray for. On some occurrences, we may be lost for words when it comes to talking to God, and that's where the Holy Spirit steps in to assist us. Romans 8:26 reads:

> Likewise, the Spirit also helps our infirmi-
> ties: for we know not what we should pray for as
> we ought: but the Spirit itself makes intercession
> for us with groanings which cannot be uttered.

The Holy Spirit will lead us and guide us into the proper way to make our petitions known unto God. The Spirit knows how God, the Father, desires for us to talk to him. On our own, we might say meaningless and vain words that will not profit or benefit us, but with the Holy Spirit's divine guidance, we will approach God with sincere words that move God to intervene in our behalf.

The Spirit assists us and helps us to truly communicate with God. The Holy Spirit is virtually speaking for us, or as one might say, on our behalf. As children of God, it's important to know that God's eyes are upon the righteous, and his ears are open unto their cry (Psalms 34:15).

The Holy Spirit knows just what we need. It is very capable of separating and discerning our wants from our needs. It brings immediate attention to the things that are most important. The Spirit also utters words for us that our fleshly nature cannot comprehend or present to God. When we don't know exactly what to say, the Holy Spirit takes over.

During our quiet time with God, we should not fail to tell him everything that's on our minds. Don't try to hide anything from him. Be honest with the Lord. Don't be afraid to open up to him and even disclose our deepest thoughts. His word says in Job 42:2, "I know that you can do everything, and that no thought can be withheld from you." In his omniscient nature, he knows what we're thinking.

Remember, he knows our secrets, actions, and behaviors; therefore, we should ask God to forgive us of all of our trespasses and daily sins that we commit against him.

It is always wise to confess our sins and tell the Lord that we are truly sorry for those sins that we have committed against him and ask him for forgiveness. In asking for forgiveness, please do so with Godly sorrow and a remorseful heart. In 2 Corinthians 7:10, it reads: "For Godly sorrow worketh repentance to salvation not to be repented of: but the sorrow of the world worketh death."

I'm so thankful that when we repent, not only does God forgive us, but he also places our sins in the "sea of forgetfulness" and remembers them no more (Micah 7:18–19). Please consider the "power" of *true repentance*, for it moves our God to forgive us of our most serious of transgressions.

James 4:8 reads: "Draw nigh to God and He will draw nigh to you." What that really means is that we become closer to our Lord, spiritually and emotionally, through daily and meaningful devotionals. He draws nigh (comes near to us) in response to our coming close to him by sincerely seeking him with an upright walk. As we draw close to him, our relationship with God becomes very personal and seriously intimate; for in our precious time in his face, we become more like Christ, which is his desired goal for each of us.

The songwriter penned these words, "I come to the Garden alone," and that's where we find Jesus, alone in the garden of Gethsemane. As usual, the Lord came to a *solitary* place to pray. He desired to be alone in talking to the Father. Therefore, he ventured into a familiar environment where he often visited (*Gethsemane*). He was at a very crucial *crossroad* in his life, and he truly needed the Father's intervention.

It was very vital that he would enquire of God for instructions and direction concerning the upcoming events. In order to please the Father, it was very important that he would seek his guidance. He was led by the Spirit to visit the Mount of Olives, which was the place called *Gethsemane*.

I'm reminded of a certain situation in the scriptures where Joshua, the servant of the Lord, made a decision concerning a matter without consulting God. During previous times in his life where certain decisions had to be made, he would always inquire of God as to what to do. However, during this particular time, for whatever the reason, he decided not to inquire of God. Because of his ill-advised choice of not consulting God during their pilgrimage to the promised land, he and the children of Israel were deceived and tricked into a peace covenant with some of the inhabitants of the surrounding lands (Joshua 9:1–27).

Oh, the price we pay when we fail to involve God. Things we deem as small and meaningless matters can easily become huge mistakes when we don't consult God concerning all situations. This lack of discernment was the only recorded flaw in Joshua's leadership of God's people. At all times, before we act, please consult God!

As we return to the garden scene, we find Jesus searching for answers. In knowing of the importance of the almighty's guidance and instruction, he realized that he needed to hear from the Father. In that lonely but anointed *garden* (Gethsemane or the Mount of Olives), he confronted his most daring and trying temptation to that point in his life. His actions in the garden are recorded in Matthew 26:36–46, (Mark 14:32–42, (Luke 39–46, and John 18:1–2.

In the "pressing place," he found an answer and a solution to *his dilemma*. It is imperative to note that not only did the Lord inquire of the Father, but he remained there in the garden until the reassurance of his mission was spiritually confirmed. Never get in a hurry, dear hearts. Always wait for an answer and confirmation from the Lord.

It is very foolish and vain to ask God for an answer, direction, and council, and not wait for God to respond to your request. Acting hastily without waiting on God could be a matter of financial and social detriment, and possibly, even a matter of life and death. In 1 Samuel 30:1, before David pursued his enemies, he inquired of God. God faithfully responded to David's request, and by him patiently waiting on the Lord, he was able to recover his family, all his goods, and the enemy's belongings as well.

However, in sharp contrast, King Saul made several hasty decisions without consulting God, and it cost him the *kingship*, rejection by God, and eventually his life and also the lives of his sons (1 Samuel 13:1–14).

Jesus, as I mentioned earlier, on the night that he was betrayed, went as he often did to the Mount of Olives (Gethsemane). And according to John 18:1–2, Judas, one of the twelve, knew where he was. Judas knew where to find Jesus because he often went to the garden of Gethsemane with his disciples to pray. Judas probably said to the Sanhedrin and the Roman soldiers, "I know where he is. He's at the Mount of Olives, for he goes there all the time to pray."

I believe the enemy knows the children of God's *prayer rooms, prayer lives,* and *prayer partners*. When you have a special and anointed prayer life and relationship with the Lord, the *enemy* is well aware of it. For as the *enemy* knows the *holy one,* he also knows his followers.

I wonder, does anyone know your prayer life and your prayer routine? Does anyone know of the certain times of the day in which you are seeking God in prayer? Do you have certain times of the day in which you retreat to your *solitary place* for intimate time with God? Those times are *priceless*.

I'm here to say to you, dear hearts, make no decisions without God. Most of our important decisions require time and serious thought. Jesus went to the garden the night of his betrayal to pray to the Father. He would pray that his will would somehow override God's will for his life. On that night in the garden, he took with him Peter, James, and John, the *inner circle*, which were those closest to him. He took these along with him that they might comfort and encourage him as he prayed and would seriously pray with him and for him.

Judas knew where he was. Judas knew, by acquaintance and observation, that Jesus was a praying man. And he knew of the place where he often prayed. We at times should, as Jesus did, have *prayer partners* (*prayer warriors*) to strengthen and encourage us.

The people whom we can count on to pray with us and for us are our *prayer partners*, and not just any ole prayer partner, but ones with whom we believe can get a prayer through to God. Men and women who understand the power and effectiveness of intercessory prayer are always sought out during tough and trying times; therefore, he took along with him the *inner circle, his prayer warriors*, for he desperately needed their spiritual support.

He needed strength to fulfill God's will for his life. He realized that he needed additional praying power from others. In Luke 22:39–46, he says to Peter, James, and John, "Pray that you enter not into temptation." He wanted them to pray that the *enemy* would not gain an advantage on them through their spiritual weakness. We should always pray that the temptation from the *enemy* does not hinder the divine effectiveness of our prayers through unbelief and doubt, for it is wise to be aware of the destructive forces of the *spiritual attacks* we face from the *devil* each and every day.

Jesus said to them, "Watch with me one hour while I pray." In other words, he tells them to seriously pray with him as he sincerely prayed to the Father. He was telling them that he needed their undivided attention in praying with him. He wanted them to watch (intercede) for him as he went to a space from them to pray.

I'm curious as to whether you have any friends that you can count on to seriously take up their prayer mantle and pray with you about the most important issues in your life. Intercessory prayer partners are extremely helpful and very important as we wrestle against spiritual wickedness in high places (Ephesians 6:12).

He says to them, "Pray with me one hour." Some may think that an hour is an unusual long amount of time to pray, but when one is used to *quality* and *crucial* prayers, an hour or so becomes mere routine. It does seem that an hour of prayer was a bit too long for these disciples, for when Jesus returned from praying the first time, he found them asleep. In his response to their drowsiness, he rebuked them for not being able to stay awake. He says, "What, could you not watch with me one hour?"

Again, he leaves them to go away to pray, hoping that they would, at least, this time pray along with him.

In his first prayer journey, He requested that the Father remove that dreaded cup of death from Him. Even in his strength as the Son of God in *majesty* and *power*, yet in his flesh, he was weak and did not want to die. Through the weakness of the flesh, he did not want to endure the impending pain and agony of the cross, for he, being the Son of God, knew what gloom was rapidly approaching him within the next few hours and the following day.

During his prayer that night, he struggled in his flesh, as we all do. Having already requested twice that the bitter cup be removed from him, he yet continues to struggle with his appointed mission. He comes to his disciples the second time, and lo and behold, he finds them asleep again.

Nevertheless, he goes away a third time to pray as beforehand. However, on this third trip, *divine* intervention takes over. The Bible tells us that an angel comes to strengthen him to succumb to the will of God and allows his own will to be defeated, realizing that for this cause, he came into the world to die for the sins of the whole world.

As he prayed in *agony* for his will to be defeated, the Bible states that sweat fell from his body as great drops of blood. In his agony, *supplication* was manifested and truly evident, for the painful emotions of having his will defeated, spiritually crucified the flesh, in so doing, the sweat and tears fell as great drops of blood. In his supplication, his words were probably too painful to utter, and his eyes burned as the tears, literally ran dry.

In supplication, tears painfully run down one's face. Words become too painful to utter. Supplication is *spiritual agony* that crucifies the flesh and allows the spirit to prevail; thus giving over to total surrender to God's will. For Jesus to die to self-will in order to please God is simply breathtaking and remarkably amazing.

Now in the *divine presence* of Jehovah at Gethsemane, God's will prevailed, and his will is defeated. He's now ready to fulfill his mission. He's now determined to give his life for the sins of the whole world. He's now willing to pay sin's debt and restore mankind's relationship with the almighty God by sacrificing his sinless body as a ransom and propitiation for your sins and mine (1 John 4:10). Gethsemane was the spiritual battlefield where Jesus struggled to succumb to the will of God.

Gethsemane was the place where the sacrificial animals were kept the day before the Passover festival. The quiet garden is where the Lord Jesus, the perfect and sinless sacrificial lamb, spent his last hours before his brutal beating and humiliation at the heartless hands of the Roman soldiers. Gethsemane, the *pressing place*, the *preparing place*, the place of *spiritual agony*, the true cleaning-up room, the final place of solace and determination to defeat his will and to please the Father and accomplish his divine mission—*the agony of Calvary's cross!*

Please allow God to lead you to *Gethsemane*, the place where he can *empty* you of all of your desires and spiritually *fill* you with his divine will.

Need an *answer, direction, guidance, strength,* and *faith* to do his will? You can find it all at *Gethsemane, the pressing place!*

3

He's in the Mountains

It's very important that we spend time with God, not just mere meaningless moments but rather quality time. A lot of people may pray a lot, but how much *quality time* do they spend with God? Quality time compared to the *quantity* of time really makes a difference in your relationship with the Lord.

My dear friends, we need to take time out to not only pray but to sincerely and seriously seek God. We must deem it extremely crucial to make time to pray. Some, I've found to believe, have no time for precious *quality prayer*.

One might ask, just what is *quality* prayer? I believe that *quality prayer* is not just mere routine words uttered, "Now I lay me down to sleep, I pray the Lord, my soul to keep," but quality prayer is deep, intimate, sincere, and serious conversation with the Lord. It's very meaningful, honest, and truthful words shared with God concerning you and your circumstances.

Remember, it's not always about how long one prays, but rather, it's about what one says to God in prayer and the effect it has on the individual's relationship with God and the response one receives from him.

Jesus often climbed into the mountains to pray, for he truly needed his father's strength, comfort, and guidance. In fact, his consistent prayer life (climbing into the mountains) demonstrated his wholesome need for God's *divine* intervention in every aspect of his earthly life. He visibly and openly portrayed to his disciples a consistent pattern of daily prayer.

Is your everyday life ever interrupted by specific times when you step away from the daily routines of life to engage in quiet conversation with God? Jesus demonstrated throughout his life on earth the importance of daily *intimacy* with God.

His disciples had a hands-on view of his modeled life of consistent and continual prayer. His times in the mountains, wilderness, garden, and other places praying became mere routine occurrences. They watched him as he would often *leave them behind* and go into *seclusion* to be alone with God.

Oh, what a testimony! He set an example by his prayer life of how to get very close to God and gain his attention and responses when needed. I'm sure he could literally say to his followers, "Don't just do as I say, but do as you see me do." Saying to them, "As often as you see me pray, it would be very beneficial to you if you would follow my example."

One might even ask why would Jesus climb into the mountains or go to other destinations to pray? He needed to, at times, get away from the crowds that thronged him and the many, many distractions surrounding him and *just be alone with God.* To get away from the hustle and bustle of life and meditate and concentrate on the mission set before him was of top priority. This required *mountain time* alone with God. Luke 5:16 reads, "And he withdrew himself into the wilderness and prayed."

I know that corporate prayer is good and very much needed in its own proper place, for there is always strength in numbers. We know from God's word that if one can chase a thousand, then two can put ten thousand to flight (Deuteronomy 32:30) and where two or three are gathered together in his name, he's in the midst (Matthew 18:20).

God honors the saints praying together in unity during certain times. In no way am I trying to discredit or belittle the necessity or importance of unified corporate prayer, for it's very vital to the work of the body of Christ, but there are times when one needs their intimate time alone with God, for certain things need only to be spoken to God. Even certain conversations need to be discussed only between yourself and the almighty God.

Some secretive information is only to be shared in quiet settings where words will never be echoed throughout the land but kept in confidence with God. My friends, some words and experiences are not deemed wise to be shared with everyone or in open setting, not even to be shared with our closest brothers and sisters in Christ. Intimate matters need only God's *attention*. We should trust God at all times, knowing that when one tells him secret things, he tells no one.

Mark 6:46 reads, "And when He had sent them away, He departed into a mountain to pray." Jesus made it a mandate to get away from *folk* and take some time to be alone in spiritual solitary confinement. This was a regular routine for him during his time here on earth.

When I think of being alone with God, I'm reminded of Jacob, the patriarch. The Bible tells us that Jacob had a serious dilemma, and he, most desperately, needed God's *intervention*. God purposefully arranged the situation in order that Jacob could be left all alone, for the Lord desired an "intimate encounter" with Jacob (Genesis 32:24–30).

A few of those verses tell us that Jacob was left alone, and there wrestled a man with him until the breaking of day. That man was the angel of God. It was actually the almighty God in angelic form, commonly known to theologians as a *theophany*.

Jacob would have never experienced this *supernatural encounter* with God had he not been left alone. Because he was left alone, he was able to feel, handle, and touch the *intangible, omnipotent,* and *incredible* God. This glorious privilege was not allowed to any other biblical characters (truly amazing!).

Moses, on many occasions, spent quality time in God's face. It's recorded in scriptures that on two of these occasions, he remained in the *presence* of God for forty days and forty nights (Exodus 24:1–18, 34:1–35).

The scriptures tell us in (Exodus 34:29) that because Moses spent so much time in God's face, when he came down from the mountains, the people noticed that his face literally shined. That's exactly what happens when you spend *quality* time with God—your face and entire demeanor is enlightened by the presence of the Lord.

We *shine* because of his *radiant light*. There's just something uniquely different and special about *praying folk*. It's in the mountains; for there, one receives a *radiant glow* and a *special* enlightening because of being in the presence of Jehovah.

King Jehoshaphat was in trouble. The enemy was all around Israel, threatening their survival and existence. He needed an answer. The people needed God's immediate help. So, what did the king do? He and the Israelites prayed unto God and asked God for help (corporate prayer). Because they sought the Lord, he heard and answered their prayers, delivering them from their enemies (2 Chronicles 20).

Jehoshaphat knew where the answer was. The only answer is always in God's face. He knew he could reach God through prayer. Jehoshaphat looked to the hills, because, like King David, he realized that all of his help came from the Lord (Psalm 121:1–2).

Peter was kept in prison, intended to be killed after Easter by Herod, the Roman king. The Bible declares that prayer was made without ceasing by the saints (Acts 12:1–17). God heard their sincere, urgent, and persistent prayers. As a result, Peter was delivered by divine intervention from the deadly hands of the Roman ruler.

Intercessory prayers are very much needed in our struggles through this life. These intercessory prayers are those rendered unto God by others on our behalf. We all need as much spiritual help and assistance that we can get. My prayers along with the fervent effectual prayers of righteous friends avail much and have a lot of influence on our God reacting to our circumstances (James 5:13–16).

Some of us have such a wonderful prayer life. Because of that unique prayer life, I believe that even *angels* take notice of our deep reliance on God, and believe it or not, others take notice as well.

Enoch was such a righteous man and had such an unbelievable relationship with God, insomuch the Lord did not allow him to see death; for the Bible says, God took him. In Genesis 5:18–24, it is written that Enoch walked with God for three hundred years, and I believe that the way he walked with God those three hundred years was on his knees. He, like Moses, had such a relationship with the almighty. Enoch stayed *in the mountains* with God. For he knew that in order to be extremely close and intimate with God, he needed devoted and dedicated time in his face.

Hebrews 11:6 reads, "But without faith it is impossible to please Him: for he that comes to God must believe that He is, and that He is a rewarder of them that diligently seek Him." I believe I have what the Bible calls a *gift of faith* (1 Corinthians 12:1–9). I also believe this gift is often manifested. On one occasion, I was asked where do I receive my seemingly great faith? They wondered, was it from my mother or a family member or even, perhaps, a friend or some life-changing experience? My reply was that my faith in God comes from a fervent study of God's word and, most of all, my intimate quality time in God's face (*it's my prayer life that enhances my faith*).

I'm constantly approaching him and sharing my deepest secrets and thoughts with the one who knows me best. When I'm with him, I'm diverging in real serious conversations, talking to him as though he's my closest of friends, and truthfully speaking, he is. Being open with him in solitary prayer has totally and completely strengthened my relationship with God. Allowing his divine presence to *spiritually overwhelm* me has produced a great change in my life.

Seeking him for guidance, telling him about all my troubles, and sharing secret thoughts has helped me to deal with my spiritual shortcomings. No matter how small or great they may seem to be, he has helped me to overcome many sinful circumstances and dilemmas because I confide in him. He's always encouraging and admonishing me in his word. Through my prayer life, I'm encouraged to cast all of my cares upon him, for he cares for me (1 Peter 5:7). The songwriter pens these words, "I must tell Jesus all about my troubles, for He's a very constant friend!"

It's hard for one to talk about the answer to a situation without having an experience of overcoming great obstacles through a relationship with God in prayer. If you've never experienced it, then you simply don't know the joy and relief of him coming to your rescue.

If you've endured, through time and patience, certain problems, you are persuaded and will be assured of who brought you out.

Because you've consulted with the *master* and have seen him at work, then you can truthfully testify of God's miraculous delivering power.

I'm reminded of a story I once heard about wild geese flying over an area where a pond was. They descended from the skies, preparing to set their feet in the refreshing waters below just to find food and rest. While they were descending, gunshots rang out from the hunters hiding in the bushy terrain surrounding the pond.

As the geese hear the sounds of gunshots, they begin to ascend to the skies toward the heavens. They continue to ascend upward into the skies until they can no longer hear the sounds of gunfire.

That's what we need to do when we hear the enemy's spiritual gunfire and attacks determined to harm us. We need to rapidly ascend into the spiritual mountains unto God until we no longer hear the enemy's gunfire of hatred, slander, clamor, ridicule, cruel mocking, and persecution.

True believers have always ascended upward into the heavens where God is. They were so *high in the sky* that the enemy's arsenal of spiritual attacks had *no effect* on their lives or their relationship with the Lord. It would be very beneficial to our walk with God if we would allow God to *hide* us in the *sanctuary*. Just being able to go into the *house* of God to pray would be like a *shield* protecting us from spiritual *demons* (Psalm 27:4–5).

Yes, dear friends, he's surely in the valley, but there's real distractions in the valley. But *in the mountains* where God abides, distractions cease. They no longer hinder our much-needed communication with him. Jesus knew where the answer was. The *answer* is always in the *solitary place*, alone with God.

An old adage says, "much prayer, much power; little prayer, little power; no prayer, no power."

Be determined to take the time out to climb into the mountains to get away from life's many distractions and find God, for *he's in the mountains*.

4

Persistent Prayer

Peter and John made it a mandate to venture to the temple every day at the hour of prayer (Acts 3:1). A lame man received healing because of their faithful and constant desire to please God by coming to the house of God. Had they not faithfully come to the temple, this miracle would not have taken place, and the lame man would not have had a testimony to tell of God's power.

While coming to the temple on a regular basis, we must have patience and not grow weary in doubt, because we haven't received the answers to our request. James 1:2–4 reads:

> My brethren, count it all joy when ye fall into divers temptations; knowing this, that the trying of your faith worketh patience but let patience have her perfect work, that ye may be perfect and entire, wanting nothing.

Remember, God never loses his power to bless. The trials and tribulations we may encounter will certainly produce patience, for they are designed to help us have special strength and enable us to wait on God. Just keep coming faithfully to him and believe. It will eventually render the desired results.

Hebrews 10:35–37 reads:

> Cast not away therefore your confidence, which hath great recompense of reward. for ye have need patience, that, after ye have done the will of God, ye might receive the promise. for yet a little while, and He that shall come will come, and will not tarry.

We have to know and understand that God will answer at the appointed time (Job 14:14). God will show up only when he's ready to. You can't hurry *his appointed time*, but you can surely hinder and prolong it. Being disrespectful, mumbling, complaining, and doubting will certainly displease God and set your blessing further back than its original appointed due date.

In Hebrews 6:13, we learn that Abraham was promised a son in his old age. Even against insurmountable odds, he believed and trusted that God was able to perform what he had promised. He did not stagger in unbelief but waited patiently for God to fulfill his promise. Abraham knew that God cannot lie and that he would definitely do exactly what he had promised.

When God makes a promise to you, rest assured that he will fulfill what he has promised, for he is biblically and faithfully bound by his word. Lamentations 3:22–23 reads:

> It is of the Lord's mercies that we are not consumed, because His compassions fail not. they are new every morning: Great is thy faithfulness.

Titus 1:2 reads:

> In hopes of eternal life, which God, that cannot lie, promised before the world began.

I say to you, my friends, when we wait patiently, looking, hoping, and believing, in due time, we will receive the promised blessings. Genesis 18:10a reads:

> And he said, I will certainly return unto thee according to the time of life; and, lo, Sarah thy wife shall have a son.

We have an *oath of confirmation* from God, simply stating that if God has said it, then that settles it, and I believe that he will certainly do that which he has spoken, for it is impossible for him to tell a lie. Hebrews 6:17–18 reads:

> Wherein God, willing more abundantly to shew unto the heirs of promise the immutability of his counsel, confirmed it by an oath: That by two immutable things, in which it was impossible for God to lie, we might have a strong consolation, who have fled for refuge to lay hold upon the hope set before us.

Our hope in our God is the *anchor of our souls*. The beauty of our hope in God is that it keeps us praying, believing, and holding on. Through his precious word, we understand that God has a track record of faithfully doing what he has said that he would do. Because he's faithful, we are definitely assured and refuse to worry about whether he will answer our prayers.

Paul encouraged the Galatian church to not give up on God and his promises. Galatians 6:9 reads: "And let us not be weary in well doing: for in due season we shall reap if we faint not." "Due season" means that God, in his infinite wisdom, knows when it's the *best time* to bless you. His *due time* is hardly ever when we want it to be but rather when he wants things to happen. It may be tomorrow, next month, next year, or perhaps the next ten years, for due season is just that, *due season*.

The psalmist stated in Psalms 40:1–2,

> I waited patiently for the Lord; and He inclined unto me and heard my cry. He brought me up out of a horrible pit, out of the miry clay, and set my feet upon a rock, and established my goings.

Because God came through, the psalmist gave a true testimony of God's true faithfulness. He will reward us when we trust him and patiently wait on him. Isaiah 40:31 reads:

> But they that wait on the Lord shall renew their strength; they shall mount up with wings as eagles; they shall run, and not be weary; they shall walk and not faint. Isaiah continued his sincere encouragement to Israel.

Isaiah 49:23 reads:

> For they shall not be ashamed that wait for me. (Psalms 31:1; 25:1–2, 20; 71:1)

Don't give up, dear hearts; don't ever give up. In Psalms 27:7, 13–14, King David asked the Lord to help him and deliver him from his troubles. He stated that he would have given up had he not believed that the Lord would come to his rescue.

Jesus asked this question in Luke 18:8: "I tell you that He will avenge them speedily, nevertheless when the Son of Man cometh, shall He find faith on the earth?" There is one thing that is drastically declining among the saints. And that is faith in our God's ability to come through for us. When the Lord returns, shall he find faith among his believers? Remember, without faith, it's impossible to please him.

In that parable in Luke 18, the widow woman's continual coming (*her bold persistence*) *and determination* caused her to receive her answer to her request. Her "continual coming" is the theme of that entire parable. What a great lesson we should learn from this woman's determination—not to give up.

The Lord instructed Isaiah to tell the pastors to continue to encourage the people. He admonished them to never hold their peace but rather boldly proclaim that the Lord is very faithful and would indeed rescue them from their oppressors. The Lord vividly challenged Isaiah and the men of God to compel the children of Israel to "give the Lord, absolutely, no rest" and to tell them to worry him until he established them as his blessed and chosen people (Isaiah 62:1–12).

I believe what the Lord was saying to the people is that they should literally trouble him over and over, again and again. He wants us to weary him and continue to stay in his face until he answers. Remember the widow woman's *continual coming*!

She never gave up. She believed that if she just kept coming, the unjust judge would see her boldness, persistence, and unquenchable faith and would then grant her request. Our God is basically trying to reveal something about him to all of his children. He is telling us, through his word, that if we would show him our great confidence in his faithfulness by our holding on and not giving up, it would cause him to bless us, even though it may be a long time in taking place.

My son, Michael, at four years old, asked me to buy him a bicycle. I promised him that I would get the bike for him. I told him that I was going to purchase it in a week or two.

Well, the next day, he asked me again for the bicycle. I again told him that I would get the bike. I was surprised the next day, as I returned home from work, by an enthusiastic little four-year-old waiting for me with the same question, "Daddy, where is my bicycle?" He also added these convicting words, "Daddy, you promised me that you would get me a bicycle. You promised, and I know you are going to get me my bike because you promised."

I was totally ashamed and convicted because I had not done what I had promised; after all, I was his father, and he reminded me of it. Because of his eagerness, persistence, and belief that I was able to get him his bike, I succumbed to determined faith and immediately went to the store and got him his request (his bicycle), for after all, I was his father, and he was my son.

His display of strong faith, coupled with works (his continual coming), prevailed. If my son could show me just how bad he really wanted his bicycle, then why can't we, as God's children, show our heavenly Father just how bad we want the things we ask him for.

We need to pray when we don't feel like praying. We need to PUSH (pray until something happens). That's right, my friends, until God answers, *keep praying!*

The word of God tells us to pray without ceasing (1 Thessalonians 5:17). Two notable and powerful examples of continual and persistent prayer are found in King David's and the beloved Jewish exile Daniel's prayer lives. It is recorded in scripture that these two patriots prayed at least three times a day (Psalms 55:16–17, Daniel 6:10–11).

These two biblical giants of faith were accustomed to staying in God's face. Both were regularly at the spiritual altar. They probably started their day on their knees in the presence of the Lord. Routine prayer was comely to them because they realized the importance and effects it had on their circumstances.

God wants to see just how bad you want the blessing. Because of your staggering persistence and extreme boldness, God will *marvel* and take notice of such great faith and determination and perhaps proclaim that he had never seen such a display of faith (Luke 7:9).

5

He Heard You the First Time

Sometimes we may wonder within our hearts or even ask ourselves whether or not God really hears our prayers. In 1 John 3:22, it reads, "And whatsoever we ask, we receive of Him, because we keep His commandments, and do those things that are pleasing in His sight."

Yes, God hears the cries of the righteous. For he tells us that he will hear and answer because we keep his commandments. A sure way to receive his blessings is to obey the things that he asked of us, for obedience will get God's attention right away. Just keep pleasing him with your life, and you'll have your prayers answered, according to his will.

The enemy is always trying to tempt us to question God as to whether he knows or even cares about what's going on in our lives. Proverbs 15:3 reads, "The eyes of the Lord are in every place, beholding the evil and the good." He sees your troubles. God is well aware of what's going on in our lives (Psalms 34:15). He knows, and he cares, for he's the *omniscient, all-knowing* God!

The little ship that the disciples were in was being tossed to and fro by the turbulent winds and waves of the sea. However, Jesus was on board, but he was asleep in the bottom of the ship. The disciples were in panic mode and in great despair. Being exceedingly desperate, they cried out to the Lord, saying, "Lord, don't you care that we *perish?*"

These "fleshly beings" failed to realize that the *Lord of glory* was in their midst, and that he was *Lord* even over the tumultuous waves of the sea. He arose from his sleep and spoke to the wind and waves, saying, "Peace be still," and the waves and the winds calmed down. He said to His disciples, "Oh you of little faith." They marveled with great amazement, saying, "What manner of Man is this, in that even the wind and the waves obey Him?" (Matthew 8:23–27).

Because Jesus was aboard the ship with them, there was really nothing that they should have been worried or terrified about. *He calmed the storm* in their life, and he will calm the storms in our lives as well. Please, let's cast all our cares upon him, for he cares for us (1 Peter 5:7).

Sometimes we feel like God is taking too long to answer our prayers. Because of this perception, we grow weary and seem to give up. If we could only realize that the *only wise God* really knows what he's doing. *He's just too wise to make a mistake!*

Try to remember that God's timing is not like ours, nor is it subject to our demands. With human beings, time means every time, but for God, time means absolutely nothing. With God, a thousand years is considered as but one day, and one day is considered as a thousand years (2 Peter 3:8). In the spiritual realm, forty years is merely one hour. *Wow!*

God is not controlled nor affected by the amount of time it takes to accomplish his will. God always knows the *right time* to react and respond to our troubles. At times, we may cry day and night, wondering why it's taking so long. He knows and he cares. Whatever you do, please don't give up; just trust him, be still, and know that he is God (Psalms 46:10).

Romans 8:28 reads: "And we know that all things work together for good to them that love God; those who are called according to His purpose." Be encouraged. He is working it all out for your good.

The Bible tells us of a man named Lazarus who was sick unto death, and his family needed Jesus to come to his hometown immediately (John 11:1–44). In this story, we find out that Jesus did not come right away but chose rather to linger two more days where he was, saying that the sickness was not unto death, but for the glory of God, and that the Son of God might be glorified.

While he was tarrying there where he was, Lazarus died. After several days, he comes to Bethany where Lazarus's sisters, Mary and Martha, were waiting for him. Martha exclaimed to him, "Lord, if you had been here, our brother would not have died." Jesus told her that her brother shall rise again. She replied to him that she knew he would rise again in the resurrection. Jesus said to her, "*I am* the resurrection." He then asked her where they had buried him. When they showed him the tomb, he told them to take away the stone from the grave. In response, they proclaimed, "Lord, he has been dead four days, and he stinks by now.

He says to them, "If you can believe, you shall see the glory of God." They removed the stone, and Jesus cried out, "Lazarus, come forth," and immediately, Lazarus came forth from the grave, and all that witnessed this *miracle* gave glory unto God.

The Lord was (days late) on purpose in order that God might receive *glory*. A lot of times God will purposely be late in answering your prayers in order that he should receive glory and praise due his name. This miracle performed by Jesus removed all doubt as to who had raised Lazarus from the grave. They had to proclaim, *it was no one but the almighty God* that had done this!

Please don't fret if it seems that God is uncaring simply because he's late. Just allow the almighty to receive some *glory*. When all was said and done, Lazarus was raised from the dead. Someone should proclaim with me, "Oh what a mighty God we serve!" Please, calm down and be patient. Jesus may have been late coming to Bethany, but *he heard them the first time* they asked him to come; even though late, he showed up!

Sometimes God does not answer our request right away because he is trying to prevent us from boasting and bragging about our own petty accomplishments. Whatever we are allowed to do and perform are all gifts given by God (Proverbs 27:1–2, Deuteronomy 8:10–17).

Sometimes people are notorious in boasting and bragging about what they think they've done. They are always gloating about what they think they have accomplished or who they perceive themselves to be. God cares nothing for this type of prideful behavior and distasteful demeanor.

If we are to boast, then we should make our boast in the Lord. We should be proud to boast of the Lord's goodness, his power, and his might. We should tell others that it is because of his love, mercy, and forgiveness that we have been redeemed and saved. My boasting and bragging will always be directed toward the Lord.

In 2 Corinthians 12:7–10, the Apostle Paul testified that a thorn was placed in his flesh by Satan to buffet him. This thorn was there because of Paul's many gifts to discern and understand the spiritual revelations given to him. This thorn was a great hindrance to his health and ministry. He asked God, on three different occasions, to remove this painful distraction from his body, but God refused to do so. He told Paul that his grace was sufficient for him. His request to remove the thorn was denied so that Paul would not have a boastful spirit and also to keep him in a perfect relationship with the Lord.

Because of this thorn, Paul humbled himself and depended on the Lord for his strength and *deliverance*. A person with a boastful spirit can never please God, especially in the ministry. He didn't remove the thorn but *he heard him the first time* he asked him to do so.

Finally, God may delay his answers to our request because he is trying to help us to understand that he allows the enemy, at times, to hinder the answers to our prayers. Even though he is an *omnipotent, all-powerful God*, he will allow Satan to prevent your desired blessings for a short period. Please remember that God is *sovereign*, which means that he is Lord of *heaven* and *earth* and does or allows whatever he wants to. We need to know that because of him and through him, we live and move and have our being (Acts 17:28).

He allows the devil to hold up our blessing, thus baiting the enemy into sticking his chest out in thinking that he has stopped God's plan, only to embarrass and humiliate this deceiver in the end. That's merely the nature of our God. He will allow the enemy to think that he's winning, only to show him in the end, and undeniably letting the devil know, who's really in control.

Daniel petitioned God to give him an answer concerning a certain prayer request. For weeks, there was no answer to Daniel's prayer. He was puzzled because the Lord had not answered. Finally, an angel came to him and told him that Satan's demons had hindered him for three weeks from bringing Daniel his answer. He told Daniel that Michael, the archangel, had come and helped him to overcome the enemy. He assured Daniel that even though it had taken three weeks for his answer, *God heard him the first time* he petitioned him (Daniel 9:20–23, 10:10–13).

There's an old saying, "He may not come when you want him to, but he's always on time!" Remember that God, in his all-wise sovereignty, always knows what he's doing and nothing catches him by surprise, and surely, nothing slips up on him unexpectedly. There is no such thing as a "coincidence" with God, for he knows all (Selah).

Rest assured, even though sometimes late, he heard you the first time!

6

Hindered and Unanswered Prayers

Sometimes you pray and you pray, and nothing happens. Your prayers are not answered. Do you ever wonder why? It very well could be because your prayers are disregarded or hindered because of certain behavior patterns.

This chapter is about *hindered and unanswered prayers*. There are several reasons why some prayers are hindered and even unanswered. When we pray to God, we need to be sure not to pray prayers that resemble those of the Pharisees of biblical times. Jesus called them hypocrites. Matthew 6:5 reads:

> And when thou prayest, thou shall not be as the hypocrites are: for they love to pray standing in the synagogues and in the corners of the streets, that they may be seen of men. Verily I say unto you, they have their reward.

If you're praying just to be seen or heard for your multitude of great words, your prayers are vain and not heard by God. Many pray to be praised by men for their sophisticated approach, hoping to attract attention to their cunning craftiness in the way that they disperse certain big words, rhymes, and fairy tales. Simply put, they just want to be seen and praised. Such prayers are deplorable, disregarded, offensive to God, and a waste of time.

Matthew 6:6–7 reads:

> But thou, when thou prayest, enter into thy
> closet, and when thou hast shut the door, pray
> to thy Father which is in secret; and thy Father
> which seeth in secret shall reward thee openly.
> but, when ye pray, use not vain repetitions as
> the heathen do: for they think that they shall be
> heard for their much speaking.

Repetitious prayers will not warrant an answer from God. Just saying the same ole things over and over again will, in no way, profit you. In most cases where prayers are repeated, it is because the one praying has literally ran out of things to say and then tries to impress God with a multitude of repetitive words.

Verse 8 reads:

> Be not ye therefore like unto them: for your
> Father knoweth what things ye have need of,
> before ye ask him.

Mark 11:24 reads:

> Therefore, I say unto you, what things
> soever ye desire, when ye pray, believe that ye
> receive them, and ye shall have them.

The primary focus is on believing in God to perform what he has promised; for without faith, it is impossible to please him (Hebrews 11:6). We need to pray the prayer of faith in all of our circumstances. If you don't add faith to prayer, then don't bother praying. *You've got to believe!*

Another reason that we at times don't receive answers to our prayers is because we limit God. Psalms 78:41 reads: "Yea, they turned back and tempted God, and limited the Holy One of Israel." We limit God when we choose to believe that he's only able to do certain *small* things but cannot perform the seemingly *impossible things*. I'll have you know that God has no problem performing the miraculous; for there is nothing too hard for God to accomplish (Job 42:2; Jeremiah 32:17, 27).

Because we limit God, he virtually limits himself. When we say that he can't do it, then he won't do it. No one wants to be deemed a failure. The mere thought of God being a failure is blasphemous. We strongly offend him and humiliate his character and even mock his great power when we question his ability to come through for us.

Husbands, let us be very careful and cautious as to the way we treat our wives. We are reminded in God's word that our prayers go unheard when we abuse our wives. In 1 Peter 3:7, it reads: "Likewise, ye husbands, dwell with them according to knowledge, giving honour unto the wife as the weaker vessel, and as being heirs together of the grace of life; that your prayers be not hindered." God instructed us to love our wives as Christ loved the church and gave his life for it. We are admonished to love our wives as our own flesh. Remember, no man ever hated his own flesh but nourished and cherished it, for he that loves his wife loves himself.

We should never treat our wives as lesser beings or second-class citizens. God forbid, if we would dare to ever treat them as common slaves. Let us remember that we don't own them, and they are our *equal partners* in the *covenant agreement of marriage*.

We should never, at any time, be abusive. I'll have you know, God is greatly displeased when one is verbally, mentally, emotionally, sexually, or physically abusive to their wives. Husbands, if you are engaged in this awful and ungodly behavior, then don't even bother praying, for your prayers are getting no further than the ceiling (Selah).

As I continue in this discourse, I'm reminded that the word says, "We have not because we ask not" (James 4:2). We don't receive because we simply don't ask! God will not answer us if we fail to ask him. A lack of faith and pride will sometimes cause us not to ask for the needed help from God. The enemy will even try to deter us by telling us that God will not answer our prayers because we've done way too many bad things.

Some may wonder whether or not God hears sinners' prayers. God will hear a sinner's prayer. If not, then none of us would be saved. John 9:31 reads: "Now we know that God does not hear sinners: but if any man be a worshipper of God, and will do His will, He hears him." God's will is for us to *repent* and walk upright; then, he will hear us.

Please be careful in displaying your demeanor and bad attitude before God; remember, it's your *attitude* that will determine your *altitude*. We should always leave our pride and arrogant spirit at the door when approaching the Lord. All of us should come before God humbly, lowly, and full of gratitude.

Prayer requests are often hindered or ignored when we come before him with the wrong kind of attitude. Israel provoked God to anger on many occasions during their wilderness experience. Their gross lack of appreciation and forward mouths tempted God to literally destroy most of them. Time after time, Moses interceded of their behalf, pleading with God not to totally wipe them out.

They were dissatisfied with the way that God was providing for them, and they often reminded him of their dissatisfaction. God angrily told Moses that he would give the complaining Hebrews meat to eat instead of the manna that they were eating daily.

They failed to realize that God, in his all-knowing wisdom, knew what he was doing and that, at the appropriate time, he would give them their heart's desire. Instead of being patient, grateful, and appreciative, they aroused his anger with their *forward remarks* and ungrateful attitude.

Psalms 78:18–19 reads: "And they tempted God in their heart by asking meat for their lust. yea they spoke against God; they said, can God furnish a table in the wilderness?"

How dare they disrespect the Lord in such a way? That type of behavior is nothing more than spiritual suicide! The mere audacity to even think of talking to God in that manner is extreme foolishness. Obviously, they failed to realize or perhaps did not understand that our God is a *consuming fire*! (Hebrews 12:29).

Please note, dear hearts, that it is a fearful thing to fall into the hands of the living God (Hebrews 10:31). The very last thing anyone wants to do is to make the Lord angry. Nahum 1:6 reads: "Who can stand before his indignation? And who can abide in the fierceness of his anger?" For your life's sake and soul's salvation, carefully and respectfully approach God, knowing that he owes us nothing; one might consider it's of his goodness that we even exist. Please don't be like the stiff-necked and hard-hearted Israelites who delayed their blessings because of an arrogant and ungrateful spirit.

We should know assuredly that not only is God able, but he is well able to do abundantly and exceedingly above that which we could ask or think (Ephesians 3:20).

We should be careful to thank God at all times for everything that he does for us. It grieves his Holy Spirit when we fail to show appreciation and gratitude for all the wonderful blessings he bestows upon us.

The Lord blessed ten lepers in healing them of their incurable diseases, but sadly, only one returned to say thank you. We seriously put our response and help from the Lord in the future in jeopardy when we fail to show our appreciation for his kindness and concern. A mere "thank you, Lord" will cause God to remember us when we are in need again.

Some tend to take our God for granted. Many just expect him to help because he's God, regardless of whether we say thank you or not; they may reply, "After all, he's God, and that's what he's supposed to do." That type of mentality and thinking will never get God to answer our prayers. No one likes to be taken for granted, especially our God.

Please have a thankful spirit. Tell him how much you appreciate him. Let the Lord know that we could do nothing without him. Be kind and considerate of his great mercies and compassionate spirit. Go out of your way in expressing your sincere gratitude for the little things that he does as well as the enormous blessings Psalm 92:1 reads: "It is a good thing to give thanks unto the Lord, and to sing praises unto thy name, O most High."

Finally, disobedience to God's word and his commandments will cause God to ignore our cries for help. Because of King Saul's disobedience to the commandments of the Lord, he could no longer receive a word from the Lord and answers to his prayers (1 Samuel 28:5–6). God Simply stops his ears and turns his face away from hearing the prayers of disobedient individuals. Obedience pleases God and prompts him to immediately come to our rescue. Obedience to God's will and word puts us in line to have God hear our prayers and abundantly bless us.

There are many situations and circumstances that will hinder and prevent God from hearing and answering our prayers. If we would only be mindful of the things in our lives that grieve the Holy Spirit, then we would strive to seek his will and be determined to please the Lord in every aspect of our everyday walk.

We all want God to not only hear us sometimes but all the time. Too many today are ignorant of the laws and written commandments of the Lord. Being oblivious to the laws of God is not justification for sinful behavior. We should study God's word to show ourselves approved unto him and seek qualified teachers that will be able to open our understanding concerning God's word and will. We should seriously strive to accomplish his God-given mandates, for they are strength and life.

7

The Secret Place

Psalms 91:1 reads: "He that dwelleth in the secret place of the Most High shall abide under the shadow of the Almighty." The scriptures did not tell us to pass by or momentarily visit our place of prayer but to dwell there.

The secret place, the spiritual *prayer room*, is our solitary mountaintop where we find comfort and solace in the presence of Jehovah. In this place of both spiritual and physical isolated seclusion, we find a loving God desiring intimate conversations with his creation.

Jacob's fear of his brother Esau caused him to desperately seek the Lord for help. Genesis 32:7a reads: "Then Jacob was greatly afraid and distressed." In Genesis 32:11, he says, "Deliver me, I pray thee, from the hand of my brother, from the hand of Esau: for I fear him, lest he come and smite me, and the mother with the children." Jacob's fear for his life drove him to the secret place. God wanted Jacob to be alone with him in a solitary place of spiritual confinement. He wanted them to be *all alone* that he might comfort and console him.

He needed to assure him that he was with him to provide him with whatever he needed and to bless him. During this encounter with the almighty God, Jacob's whole life was transformed because of God's special *touch* and anointing. Even his name was changed by God, signifying God's mercy in forgiving him of past failures and bestowing on him the blessings of Abraham. Being alone with God encouraged Jacob and truly comforted him and dismissed his fear of Esau.

God is waiting for you in the secret place. It is there we find relief and strength. I continue to expound on the fact that while David was fleeing for his life from King Saul, he experienced devastation at the hands of the Amalekites when they had invaded Ziklag, burned the city, and had taken all of their families captive (1 Samuel 30:1–20).

David and his followers were painfully saddened and distressed. To make matters worse, the men were seriously considering stoning him to death. At this desperate hour in his life, David found comfort and solace in the face of his God. He knew exactly what to do. He encouraged himself in the Lord.

Having escaped time and time again from Saul's insane assault on his life, he realized that it was God that had hid him and preserved his life. He believed that if God had delivered him so many times before, he would faithfully do it again; therefore, he sought the Lord in prayer.

It was in the secret place that David perfected his strength and courage. During his early years, he attended to his father's sheep. Being alone in the hills, he learned how to play skillfully on the musical instruments. He also had a lot of time to talk with God. It was in the Judean hills he perfected his gift of writing psalms and praising the almighty.

In his secret place, he grew close with God in the daily reading of the Mosaic law and growing familiar with the ways of the Lord. He may have at first thought it punishment to have to spend all of his time caring for sheep, but later in life, he would accredit this solemn time alone with God very beneficial and crucial to his success and his relationship with the Lord.

It was there in intimate prayer, his trust and reliance on God was tremendously increased. Because of his personal relationship with the Lord, he was confident that God would fulfill his word and that he would definitely become Israel's next king.

Sometimes God has to allow trials and sufferings to come to get us to pray. Please don't wait until trouble comes before you decide to seek God. One should always have some *timbers* in heaven. What I mean by "timbers" is that we should have multiple prayers already stored up in heaven before God (Revelation 5:8). We should pray before the storm comes, asking God to prepare us for the pending devastation that may lie ahead. Remember, he's our great God, our nourisher and comforter.

One of the things that I cherish about the secret place is, one can really be open and honest with him. Because you are alone with God, there's no need of worrying whether or not anyone else hears your intimate secrets and thoughts that you've revealed to him. When being alone with God, we should tell him how we feel about every situation. Remember, he already knows. He's just waiting for us to say it. Please realize that he cannot fill you with his Spirit and holiness until he has emptied you of yourself. Be honest, tell him every single detail about yourself, get it all out! Confession is always good for the soul.

During our time with God, please remember to pray about everything. We should ask God to intervene in our relationships with our spouses, children, loved ones, and all others. We should always ask him for guidance and direction in every aspect of life. We should never make any major decisions without God's will and approval. Attitudes and characters are truly changed in the secret place. Put yourself in a position to be blessed. Get alone, away from every distraction and spend some quality time with God.

I'm reminded of an earlier time in my life when I was experiencing some seemingly harsh circumstances. I talked to a friend of mine who just happened to be a fellow minister of the Gospel. He advised me to drive out into the countryside alone and just talk to God while driving along the way. He encouraged me to just *steal away* and spend some quality time in communication with God. Thankfully, I took his advice. During these long drives alone, and not to mention accompanied by fervent prayers, my sense of thinking changed, and my relationship with God began to be more intimate.

I had sincerely developed a deeper trust in his leading, guiding, and ordering my steps (Psalm 37:23). I truly became more spiritually content and less worried about vain circumstances. Those countryside rides became my secret place. My *downtime* alone with the Lord has truly been an incredible blessing.

I must reiterate again that the enemy desperately tries to keep you from praying, for he knows your relationship with God is synonymous to your success in life. Please don't allow the world and the devil's distractions to prevent you from communication and conversation with the Lord. The *secret place*, simply stated, we can't survive without it! The *secret place*, for strength dwell there!

8

The Power of the Weapon of Prayer

Jesus said in Matthew 7:7–11,

> [Ask], and it shall be given you; seek and ye shall find; knock, and it shall be opened unto you. for everyone that [ask] receives; and he that seeks finds; and to him who knocks, the door shall be opened. or what man is there of you, whom if his son [ask] bread, will he give him a stone? or if he [ask] a fish, will he give him a serpent? if you then, being evil, know how to give good gifts to your children, how much more shall your father which is in heaven give good things to them that [ask] him?

He said that if we, as humans, care for our loved ones, giving them good things, how much more would our heavenly father give even greater things to his children that ask him. Prayer is not just a formality; it is a powerful weapon that we, the children of God, should take advantage of every day.

Many churches have gone away from prayer meetings. In most places, they no longer exist. It saddens me because these church congregations fail to realize the effectiveness of *corporate prayer*.

There's great strength in numbers. The Bible tells us in Acts 12:1–17 that Peter was placed in prison. Verse 5 says, "But prayer was made without ceasing by the saints for him." These believers came together, touching and agreeing, knowing that if two or three we're gathered together to ask a petition of the Lord, that he would grant their request (Matthew 18:19–20). They knew the power of praying together and of one accord. Because they prayed as the body of Christ, Peter was delivered from prison.

When we pray, not if we pray, we truly demonstrate to God that we believe in prayer and that we trust him to do whatever it takes to answer our petitions. As the people of God, it is *expected* of us to ask, to seek, and to knock until he shows up and *delivers* the *Peters* of this world from *spiritual prisons.*

God's word tells us that if we ask anything, in his name, he will hear us (John 14:14). In your prayer time, call on the name of the Lord Jesus, for the name of the Lord is a strong tower; the righteous run to it and are safe (Proverbs 18:10).

It's just something about the name of *Jesus*, for there is no other name like the name of Jesus. There is no other name under heaven given among men whereby we must be saved. In critical moments call on the name of the Lord, for whosoever calls on the name of the Lord shall be saved (Acts 2:21).

There are times when we may succumb to temptation because we do not allow God to intervene. The enemy knows the effectiveness of righteous prayers; therefore, he desperately tries to distract you and keep you from praying. He has found out from the examples of so many praying biblical characters that God showed up with deliverance when they fervently prayed. Because they used their powerful weapon of prayer, they received the victory. The very last thing the devil wants you to do is pray, for when you pray, things happen.

Jesus said to Peter, "The devil desires to sift you as wheat, but I've prayed for you that your faith fail you not" (Luke 22:40). Peter was able to endure the tough times because the Lord prayed for him. Our friends and loved ones would overcome countless obstacles in life if the righteous would simply use their power and pray (James 5:13–16).

Intercessory prayer is both important and powerful. Romans 8:26 reads: "Likewise the Spirit also helpeth our infirmities: for we know not what we should pray for as we ought: but the Spirit itself maketh intercession for us with groanings which cannot be uttered."

To add noted strength to the importance of intercessory prayer, we find Moses using intercessory prayer unto God on behalf of the Israelites. He seriously prayed and asked God to forgive them of their rebellious and disobedient behavior. Because of his righteous relationship with God, he was able to convince the Lord not to destroy them (Numbers 14:10–20).

Paul desired that the early church would seriously pray for him and the other apostles, knowing that their prayers would help them carry out God's will in proclaiming the gospel to the gentile nations. In 1 Thessalonians 5:25, it reads: "Brethren, pray for us. The Apostle Paul knew that there wasn't too much they could do alone without the assistance of fellow believers praying on their behalf. Because others prayed for them, God faithfully intervened."

King Hezekiah knew the power and effectiveness of righteous prayer. When Judah's enemies invaded the land determined to conquer the Israelites, he responded to their threats by going into the house of God and spreading their intimidating letter before his God. In his urgent prayer, he reminded the Lord that they, the Jews, were his people and that the Assyrians were trying to take them into captivity. He knew that if he could just *tell the Lord*, then everything would work out fine, and God would fight against their enemies (Isaiah 37).

In times of fearful and desperate situations, use your *power* and pray. Just imagine this, we have a powerful weapon attached to our side, and we're running from the enemy—unbelievable and simply amazing! When all else fails, use your weapon. *Pray!* For he's a very present help in time of trouble (Psalm 46:1).

9

The House of Prayer

The Lord says, come into his house. He told Isaiah to tell the stranger and the eunuch who keep his word and love him, that they are welcomed in his holy temple. He says, "My house shall be called a *house of prayer* for all people" (Isaiah 56:1–7).

Do we really realize the spiritual importance of God's house? We should understand that the Lord desires to *tabernacle* with his creation. He desires for his people to abide in his presence. Wherefore, he comes down to earth and dwells with us in the tabernacle, our *house of prayer*.

The *house* of God is in the midst of our communities and neighborhoods. The *temple* is there for a divine purpose. The church building allows us to come in and worship and praise the Lord, hear the preached word, and learn more about his statues and his commandments. We also find comfort and solace within those precious walls.

Micah 1:2–3 reads:

> Hear, all ye people; hearken, O earth, and all that therein is: and let the Lord God be witness against you, the Lord from His holy temple. for, behold, the Lord cometh forth out of His place, and will come down, and tread upon the high places of the earth.

God desires to be among us, and he usually does this by coming down into the sanctuary and making his presence known.

The Lord appeared to Moses at the door of the tabernacle, the moving church in the wilderness (Exodus 33:7–11; Numbers 12:5, 16:19, 17:41–43). The *ark of the covenant* was placed in the tabernacle, representing the *presence of the Lord*. God commanded the Israelites to erect a tabernacle in order that his presence would always be with them as they journeyed through the wilderness. Years later, as they entered the promised land, this tabernacle was dissolved, and the ark of the covenant rested in a tent behind curtains.

David, in his love for God, desired to build a permanent house for God to dwell among his people. David knew the importance of having God near them. Yes, King David desired to build this holy *temple*, but it was not in the will of God. Because David was a man of war and had shed much blood, he was not allowed to construct the Lord's house.

Solomon, David's son, was granted the privilege and honor of erecting this splendid *wonder of the world*. Solomon, along with his father, wanted to build God a *magnificent edifice*. They knew that almighty God deserved the very best. Deliver me from those who would even dare to throw up a *chicken coop* and call it the house of God. God certainly deserves better than a *meager* dwelling place. After all, he is the *almighty*!

The Lord told Haggai, the prophet, to command the returning exiled Jews to rebuild the temple (Haggai 1:2–9). The Lord rebuked them and challenged them to do their very best in restoring the house of God. He warned them to consider their ways. He reminded them of how disrespectful they were to God in living in their nice ceiled houses while the house of God laid in wasteful ruins.

It seems as though some want the finest of things for themselves and the *feebler* of things for God. For we've got things backward; we should put God first in our lives, always desiring to give him our *very best*.

The Lord commanded Haggai to compel these Jews to climb the mountains and cut timber and build the Lord a house of worship. He reminded them that because of their lack of concern for

God's house, their possessions of gold and silver was blown on and taken away. They suffered great losses because of their gross disrespect for God's desires concerning his house. They lacked the *zeal* of King David in desiring to restore and beautify the temple. Psalm 69:9 reads: "For the zeal of thine house hath eaten me up; and the reproaches of them that reproached thee are fallen on me."

When we give God the best of our gifts and services, then he gives us the very best of his. Even though we know that a house made with hands cannot contain our God (1 Kings 8:27), it should be our desire that his presence dwells with us in the *house of prayer*.

So, Solomon built the temple, and the people were so excited and very happy that God finally had a permanent *dwelling place* among them (1 Kings 8).

The Bible tells us that when Solomon and the people had dedicated the temple, the *shekinah glory* of the Lord filled the house. This glory was the ultimate expression of God's presence among his people. This presence was similar to his appearance when he came down and talked with them on Mt. Sinai.

We should hunger and thirst for his shekinah glory to meet us in the temple. When we can truly feel the presence of the Lord, it literally captures us and overwhelms us to the point that all of our so-called order of service is done away with. Because of the *glory* of God entering the temple, the priest was not able to minister. When I visit churches, I'm hoping that I can *feel God*, in contrast to just *feeling good* (1 Kings 8:10–11).

When we offer the sacrifice of praise from our lips and true worship through righteous living, he receives it as a *sweet-smelling savor*, thus causing him to *joyfully* come into the house.

God is truly depending on the ministers of the Gospel to exemplify Godliness along with our praise in order that our *adoration* of him, in worship, will be sincere and not sneered upon, understanding that such Godly character is pleasing and causes him to enlighten our services with his presence.

Psalms 127:1 reads: "Except the Lord builds the house, they labour in vain that build it: except the Lord keep the city, the watchman waketh but in vain." We should want God to build the house.

He builds it with his anointed leaders that exemplify his will through their own lives. He establishes it with his holiness, righteousness, and truth preached every Sunday. He also builds the house through our devoted and sincere prayers in seeking his presence.

We should realize that we come to the house of God to pay homage to him. We gladly thank God and praise him for his many wonderful acts and countless blessings given to us daily. In our worship of him in the sanctuary, we should be in awe of his grandeur and greatness.

When we can feel God through the presence of his Holy Spirit, we tend to leave the house of God spiritually satisfied, completely nourished by the word of God, overwhelmed, overjoyed, and richly blessed. The Lord should always be the primary focus of our praise and worship.

That's why Israel, in captivity, longed for their homeland, mainly Jerusalem, for the temple was there, signifying God's Presence. *His presence is in the house of prayer!*

As I conclude this final chapter, I would like to leave you with these few spiritual nuggets.

If one wants to know more about God, then they should go into the *house of prayer*. In God's house, we learn his ways and his will (Psalms 77:13). It's in the house of prayer, we receive instructions as to how to please God in holy living. The sanctuary is truly and spiritually beneficial to all that attend.

When we are unable to make it to the sanctuary, we are to pray toward the house of prayer as Daniel did, thus realizing that God would hear our prayers. Daniel, while in Babylonian captivity, prayed from his bedroom toward Jerusalem every day (Daniel 6:1–10).

The house of prayer should be so important that one desires to enter the sanctuary as often as possible. We should long for and gladly desire to come into his presence within the walls of the local church. It is good to have the mentality of David concerning going to the house of God. Psalms 122:1 reads: "I was glad when they said unto me, let us go into the house of the Lord."

In the Lord's house of prayer, the sanctuary, the temple of God, we find Zachariah, the priest receiving the spirit of God. It was in the temple that Isaiah saw the Lord. There, in God's presence, he repented of his sins, was forgiven, cleansed, and received his calling. So many wonderful and miraculous things happen in God's house of prayer.

Church attendance on a regular basis is very essential to one's spiritual growth and maturity. The apostles made it a mandate for the people to not forsake the assembling of themselves, as was the custom of some (Hebrews 10:25). On the first day of the week, they gathered together to praise and worship the almighty God (1 Corinthians 16:1–2).

The church house is the stable *pillar* of the community. Most of us grew up in Sunday school, Bible study, and vacation Bible school. We remember Christmas carols and Easter speeches; we partook of holy communion. At the house of God, we accepted the Lord as our personal savior. In his presence, we were baptized and received his Holy Spirit. In the Sanctuary, couples get married and are given in marriage, children are christened, funerals are performed, and community gatherings take place.

The church serves many functions in the nurturing of individuals. For without the church, there would be no knowledge of God; and without the knowledge of God, the people are destroyed (Hosea 4:6). It was a routine to be in church on Sunday mornings, Sunday nights, and Wednesday nights. People were expected and determined to go to church, for it was rarely heard of that someone was not a member of a local assembly.

Again, the Lord says in his word, "My house shall be called a House of Prayer for all people." People from all kinds of backgrounds and walks of life should feel welcomed in God's house, for genuine repentance usually begins within the friendly and loving walls of the local church, which is *the house of prayer!*

Summary

Prayer is a phenomenal asset. It's virtually impossible to properly function without it. It is a mandate for a successful relationship with God. Prayer defines the child of God, and it's essential to our pleasing God. In our everyday lives, we need prayer. All of our decisions that we make in our daily lives should not be made without God's guidance. Constant and persistent prayers to God make life's journey so much easier to endure.

I'm reminded of a story I once heard on the local radio station of two pastors' wives who were having a conversation as they were mending their husbands' pants. One of the wives told the other wife that her husband's ministry was not going very well. She said that people were leaving the church and that there was a lot of chaos and confusion between the few members that were left. She said that her husband was considering leaving the church and giving up on the ministry.

The other wife, being surprised, stated that she and her husband's ministry was going quite well. She said that there weren't a great number of members, but their ministry was being blessed. She told her that people's lives were changing, many were being healed of sickness, and the Lord was wonderfully blessing their little church.

As they continued to talk, one wife was mending the seat of the pants, and the other wife was mending the knees of the pants. Now, which ministry do you think was doing well? Was it the ministry of the wife who was mending the "seat" of her husband's pants or the ministry of the wife who was mending the "knees" of her husband's pants? Persistent prayers to God work miracles; just ask the pastor's wife.

Some really don't realize the power of sincere prayer, for prayer to God is what the devil does not want us to do, for he knows its effectiveness. When we pray, we turn over to God all of our problems and troubles. Through prayer, we are saying to the Lord, "Please intercede on our behalf." We are asking him to *handle it*. We cry out, "Lord, please help us, for we need you."

Jesus set the example for us to follow with an everyday life of consistent prayer. Through his prayer life, he was teaching us the importance of meaningful prayer on a daily basis.

There are examples throughout the Bible of a great cloud of witnesses that used prayer to their advantage. They understood that they were in a spiritual warfare against the enemy and his demon followers. They realized that they could not win this battle along without the Lord's help. They used prayer to their advantage.

For many years now, I've happily and enthusiastically found my way to a little *anointed* church in downtown Grenada called All Saints Episcopal Church. I usually start my day off at this loving and peaceful *edifice* where God's presence is truly felt. This place of worship is definitely a *house of prayer*.

I emotionally remember years ago when our little store-front church doors closed in downtown Grenada. At this little precious site, I would engage in noonday prayers daily. But now the doors were closed, and I had nowhere to go for my routine noonday prayer. What was I to do now?

As always, God had a *ram* in the bush. During several meetings with local pastors, I was blessed to meet the pastor of All Saints Episcopal Church. In our conversations, I was telling her of my unfortunate circumstance and that I did not have a regular place to pray. She informed me that their church encouraged prayer and that I was welcomed to come and pray.

Thankfully, I took her up on her offer, and I've been coming to All Saints ever since. I literally start my day off there in God's presence. My frequent daily visit(s) to the church have given me a new perspective on everyday life. My time with God within these "spiritual walls" has really strengthened my relationship with others, and not to mention bringing me even closer with our Lord Jesus Christ.

People often ask me, why do I go to the church so much? I humbly tell them that I go for *spiritual nourishment.* They don't seem to understand how and why anyone would spend so much time in God's presence. Perhaps, if they are blessed to inherit eternal life, I'll ask Moses, David, and Daniel to help me explain to them the close relationship we encounter with God when we are in the *presence of Jehovah.*

I just don't believe that I could make it without my prayer life. To me, my prayer life in God's face is more important than the water I drink. I can understand what David was saying in Psalm 42:1, "as the hart panteth after the water brooks, so panteth my soul after thee, O God." For without God, I'm nothing. I hope you can understand what I'm trying to say. Honestly, I definitely need my time with the Lord, just as a baby needs its mother's milk. I've come to realize that *prayer changes things.*

To this child of God, *prayer is truly a way of life!*

About the Author

Elder Larry Young was born in Grenada, Mississippi, in 1958. He was raised by a hardworking and praying mother who prayed to God every day. Even though much of his early life was not spent serving God, he still noticed his mother's prayer life. He had a calling on his life at an early age but refused to adhere to the calling; determined to live his life as he pleased. What he didn't realize was, his mother was praying that God would save his life. In his middle twenties, sickness found its way to his door. His life of doing things his way was over. Now, he needed the Lord. He found out very quickly that he couldn't make it without God. Sickness led him to accept his calling and seek God, like his mother did, on a regular basis. He quickly found out that God was changing his life through his routine of consistent prayer. He began to go to one of the local churches to engage in prayer with the Lord. For the last fifteen years, he has faithfully visited one of the downtown local churches. In fact, he usually starts his day off in God's face at this local assembly. At first, people would stare when they saw him entering the church early in the morning on a regular basis. They would ask him why he came to the church so often and consistently. He would respond, telling them that he needed his time with God. Some would say, "No one needs that much time with God," but Elder Young believes he needs that time with God and even more. His whole ministry evolved around his relationship with God through his prayer life. He can truly understand why Daniel and King David, the biblical characters, prayed at least three times a day. He is constantly seen at this little anointed *edifice.* Elder Larry Young has learned the *power* and effectiveness of continual prayers to the Almighty God. This *man* of God would like to encourage everyone to develop a daily prayer routine with the Lord in order to establish a tremendous and spiritual relationship with him. Elder Young says, without his prayer life, he is literally nothing and of no use to God.